NORRIE EXPLORES... ROME

Help Norrie to solve the clues on a fascinating adventure!

M·AGRIPPA·L·F·COS·TERTIVM·FECIT

World Book, Inc.
180 North LaSalle Street
Suite 900
Chicago, Illinois 60601
USA

For information about other World Book publications, visit our website at www.worldbook.com or call 1-800-WORLDBK (967-5325). For information about sales to schools and libraries, call 1-800-975-3250 (United States), or 1-800-837-5365 (Canada).

Library of Congress Cataloging-in-Publication Data for this volume has been applied for.

Norrie Explores ...
ISBN: 978-0-7166-5303-5 (set, hc.)

Norrie Explores ... Rome
ISBN: 978-0-7166-5310-3 (hc.)
ISBN: 978-0-7166-5330-1 (pf.)

Also available as:
ISBN: 978-0-7166-5320-2 (e-book)

Staff

Executive Committee
President: Geoff Broderick
Vice President, Editorial: Tom Evans
Vice President, Finance: Donald D. Keller
Vice President, International: Eddy Kisman
Vice President, Technology: Jason Dole
Director, Human Resources: Bev Ecker

Editorial
Senior Editor/Indexer: Shawn Brennan
Editor/Researcher: Lynn Durbin
Content Creator: Jenna Neely
Curriculum Designer: Caroline Davidson
Project Coordinator: Kaile Kilner
Proofreader: Nathalie Strassheim

Graphics and Design
Senior Visual Communications Designer: Melanie Bender
Senior Media Editor: Rosalia Bledsoe

Acknowledgments

Writer: Izzi Howell
Illustrator: Jon Davis

Developed with World Book by
White-Thomson Publishing LTD
www.wtpub.co.uk

Cover: Norrie artwork by Jon Davis, Advocate Art; © S.Borisov, Shutterstock

4-5 © Sergii Figurnyi, Shutterstock
6-7 © Manfred Gottschalk, Alamy Images; © RTimages/Alamy Images
8-9 © Marco Rubino, Shutterstock
10-13 © Shutterstock
14-15 © Michael Abid, Alamy Images; © Endless Travel/Alamy Images
16-17 © Vito Arcomano, Alamy Images; © Stefano Tammaro, Shutterstock
18-19 © Shutterstock
20-21 © S.Borisov/Shutterstock; © Baarssen Fokke/Alamy Images
22-23 © Dan Grytsku, Alamy Images; © Mistervlad/Shutterstock
24-25 © Stefano Valeri, Alamy Images; © Davide Trolli, Shutterstock; © Sirio Carnevalino, Shutterstock
26-27 © Shutterstock
28-29 © Hercules Milas, Alamy Images; © Valerio Meil, Shutterstock
30-31 © Jeremy Pembrey, Alamy Images; © Dmytro Surkov, Shutterstock
32-33 © Alexandre Zveiger, Alamy Images; © Yannick Luthy, Alamy Images; © Marco Rubino, Shutterstock
34-35 © RomanSlavik.com/Shutterstock; © Manfred Gottschalk, Alamy Images
36-37 © Aleksandr Medvedkov, Shutterstock; © Frank Bienewald, Alamy Images
38-39 © eye35.pix/Alamy Images; © RanaPics/Alamy Images; © S.Tatiana, Shutterstock
40-41 © Stefano Valeri, Alamy Images; © Vito Arcomano, Alamy Images
42-43 © Kirk Fisher, Alamy Images; © Inge Johnsson, Alamy Images; © Rossa di sera, Shutterstock; © Boris Stroujko, Shutterstock; © Stefano Politi Markovina, Alamy Images; © ChiccoDodiFC/Shutterstock
46-47 © Shutterstock
48-48 © Stephen Bisgrove, Alamy Images; © Shutterstock
50-51 © Shutterstock

Contents

Welcome to Rome!

Hi, I'm Norrie! I'm a puffin. I love to travel the world and explore different cities around the globe.

Today, I'm in Rome, the capital of Italy. Italy is a country on the continent of Europe. Have you ever visited Rome or Italy before?

Rome has been an important city for over 2,000 years. It was the capital of the massive and powerful Roman Empire (27 B.C to A.D. 476). Later, Rome became the center of the Roman Catholic Church. The church paid for beautiful buildings and works of art. Many of the buildings from Rome's history still stand today. Visiting the city is a little bit like traveling back in time!

Even the rooftops of Rome are historic and beautiful!

Rome lies on the banks of the Tiber River.

My grandma loved to travel ... just like me! She gave me her travel journal so that I could see all of the countries and places she explored. One of her favorite cities was Rome, because she loved history. I'm going to follow in my grandma's footsteps and retrace her route around the city. There's just one problem – the journal is old, faded, and missing some parts! Will you help me make sense of her notes and find my way around the city?

Palatine Hill

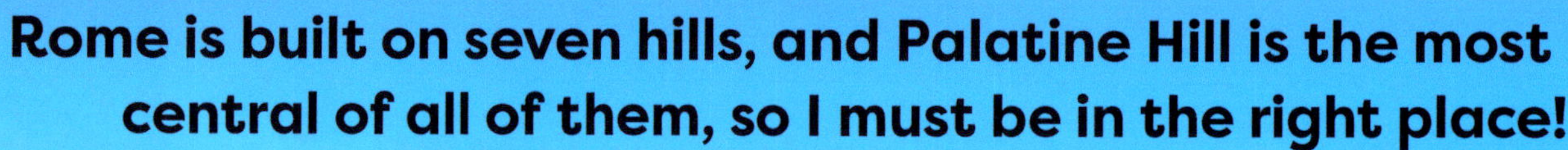

Rome is built on seven hills, and Palatine Hill is the most central of all of them, so I must be in the right place!

According to a legend, the founders of Rome, twin brothers Romulus and Remus, were looked after by a female wolf that lived in a cave on this hill. Later, Remus was killed, and Romulus became the first ruler of Rome.

Palatine Hill is one of the oldest parts of the city. In Roman times, emperors and rich people built huge villas, palaces, and temples here. The buildings were abandoned and started to fall apart after the end of the Roman Empire.

These are the ruins of the garden of one of the palaces on the Palatine Hill. It was built to look like a chariot racing track, but would have been too small for real chariots. In Roman times, the garden would have been decorated with statues and fountains.

Other buildings were built on Palatine Hill in the Middle Ages and Renaissance period. Later, archaeologists started to discover and excavate the amazing Roman buildings hidden below. Now you can explore the ruins for yourself. The villas must have been so impressive back then!

The buildings on Palatine Hill were decorated with stone carvings, painted murals, and patterned mosaic tile floors. Some of these details have survived to this day.

Roman Forum

Just downhill from Palatine Hill is the Roman Forum.

This was one of the most important public spaces in Roman times. I can't believe how many ruins there are here! I can't wait to explore. The Roman Forum was used in different ways throughout the Roman period. During the Roman Republic (509 B.C. to 27 B.C.), Rome was ruled by a government called the Senate. The senators (members of the Senate) met in a senate house here in the forum.

The Roman Forum was also home to large public buildings called basilicas, where courts were held. Official records and details of the laws of the republic were kept in the Tabularium (Hall of Records).

Later, during the Roman Empire, the forum became an important place for processions and religious ceremonies. Temples were rebuilt and new monuments, such as arches, were added. The buildings in the Roman Forum gradually crumbled after the fall of Rome. Excavations have since uncovered many of the ancient columns and arches.

The land on which the forum sits was originally a swamp! The Romans drained the area using one of their massive sewers – the Cloaca Maxima. The sewer carried water from the swamp into the Tiber River.

I've had a good look from above – now it's time to land on the ground and explore the forum on foot! There are seven temples in the Roman Forum, but there was at least one more temple that does not have any ruins remaining today. This one here was dedicated to the Roman god Saturn, who was associated with wealth. His temple was also used as a treasury to store the city's gold and silver. Inside the temple was a large statue of Saturn whose feet were tied together with wool! The wool ties were released once a year for the Saturnalia festival on December 17th.

Only eight columns remain from the Temple of Saturn. They were made of stone transported from Egypt.

Look at this massive arch! It was built in A.D. 203 to celebrate the victory of Roman emperor Septimius Severus against the Parthian Empire, which ruled over what is now Iran, Turkey, and other countries in Western Asia. The arch is covered in sculptures showing scenes from Roman battles against the Parthians. Historians believe that there used to be a massive bronze statue of Septimius Severus riding a chariot on top of the arch, but no one knows where it is today. What a mystery!

This curved wall was part of one of the most important temples in the Roman Forum. It was dedicated to Vesta, the Roman goddess of the home and the hearth (fireplace). She was also thought to protect the city of Rome. A sacred flame burned inside the temple. If the fire ever went out, it was a sign that Rome was in serious danger!

The flame was looked after by six priestesses known as Vestal Virgins. The Romans considered it a great honor to be chosen to serve as a Vestal Virgin. The priestesses often had considerable power and influence in Roman political life. They lived in the Roman Forum in a house near the temple.

That large building with the huge arches is the remains of the Basilica of Maxentius. When it was completed around A.D. 313, it was the biggest building in the Roman Forum. The Basilica of Maxentius was one of the first basilicas that had arches supporting its roof. Before that, most basilicas had columns instead.

These ruins look large, but they are actually just one side of the massive basilica. There was also a large central open space with a row of three more arches on the other side. These sections were destroyed by earthquakes in the 800's and 1300's. However, the fact that three massive arches still stand today, over 1,700 years later, shows the skill of Roman architects and builders! I wonder how many modern buildings will still be around in 1,700 years!

Colosseum

The Colosseum is one of the most famous ancient Roman buildings.

This massive amphitheater (outdoor theater) is in ruins today, but it's easy to imagine what it would have been like in ancient Roman times. Everyone in Rome, from emperors to common people, came here to watch fierce gladiator fights and wild animal hunts. Gladiators were trained warriors who fought in battles for entertainment. Sometimes, the arena would be flooded to re-enact sea battles with boats.

The Colosseum is built of brick and concrete covered with stone. After the end of the Roman Empire in Rome, the Colosseum fell out of use. Stones from the Colosseum were taken and used for other buildings around the city. Over the years, it was used as a burial ground, a fortress, housing, and a holy place for Christians. Today it is one of the world's biggest tourist sites, attracting over 6 million visitors a year. Would you like to visit?

I've chosen a popular gladiator weapon – the trident! It looks a bit like a big fork!

In Roman times, the Colosseum sat 50,000 spectators on marble and wooden benches.

You can see the hidden rooms and tunnels under the arena floor where gladiators and wild animals were kept before the show. They were brought up to the arena through elevators pulled on ropes.

The Colosseum has three stories of arches and one plain story.

Circus Maximus

There aren't any clowns here, but a Roman circus was one of the best places to go for entertainment!

A circus was an outdoor venue that usually had a racetrack with one curved end. Chariots or horses raced around the track. People sat in rows on three sides. The Circus Maximus was the largest of the ancient Roman circuses. It seated about 250,000 spectators. Its name actually means "largest circus" in Latin! People still come here to have fun, as it is used as a concert space today.

Romans went to the Circus Maximus to watch chariot races. A race day began with a musical procession of charioteers, images of the gods, and dancers and musicians. Four to six main teams of chariots raced seven laps around a central stone barrier. Moveable sculptures of dolphins or eggs served as lap markers, to indicate the progress of the race. The winner of the race received money, a laurel wreath, and a palm branch.

Crashes were common in Roman chariot races because teams were allowed to block one another. Riders carried knives to cut themselves loose in the event of a crash.

Vittoriano

The Victor that my grandma mentioned in her journal has to be King Victor Emmanuel II, the first king of a united Italy.

This monument, known as the Vittoriano, was built in his honor. Before the rule of King Victor Emmanuel II, Italy was split into many different states and kingdoms. In 1861, nearly all of the country joined together and Victor Emmanuel II became the king. However, it wasn't until 1870 that Rome finally became part of Italy.

Locals here sometimes call the Vittoriano the "wedding cake," and I can see why! Its three levels, large staircases, and rows of columns do look a bit like a cake.

The Vittoriano is built on the Capitoline Hill, another of Rome's seven hills.

It's worth climbing up the Vittoriano and exploring the many smaller statues and monuments on each level. In the center of the first level is the Tomb of the Unknown Soldier, which is dedicated to all Italian soldiers who were killed or went missing during wars. Above this is a statue of King Victor Emmanuel II riding a horse. If you make it to the top, there's a roof terrace with incredible views of Rome.

Better keep climbing then!

The bronze statue of King Victor Emmanuel II is a massive 39 feet (12 meters) high.

Pantheon

That amazing domed roof is in the center of the Pantheon.

While some Roman temples are dedicated to one god in particular, the Pantheon was meant to honor all the gods. Its name comes from the Greek word "pantheion," which means "place for all gods." Compared with many other ancient Roman buildings, the Pantheon is very well preserved because it has always been in use. Over the years, it has been used as a Christian church and a burial place for famous Italian artists and kings.

Time to head inside for the Pantheon's most famous feature – its massive domed roof! Roman architects were some of the first people to design and build huge domed roofs. They wanted the inside of the building to be open and attractive, without lots of columns in the way. They worked out how to balance the weight of the dome so that the outside walls of the building could support it. This engineering technique is still used today.

Piazza Navona

Of course, the Piazza Navona! This large square was built on top of a Roman circus.

The shape of the square follows the shape of the stadium. It's long and thin with one curved end, just like the Circus Maximus! You can take a tour of the underground ruins of the Roman circus. They are about 16 feet (5 meters) below street level. The circus was paved over in the 1400's and turned into the square I'm standing in today! It was used as the site of the main market in Rome for the next 300 years.

I'm off for a quick dip in the fountain!

If you could travel back in time and visit Piazza Navona at some point between 1652 and 1865, you might end up with wet feet! For some time between 1652 and 1866, the square was flooded on Saturdays and Sundays in August! This was part of a festival to celebrate the Pamphili family – a rich and powerful family who lived in a palace on the square.

Piazza Navona isn't flooded any more, but there is still plenty of water in its three fountains. Its most famous water feature is the Fountain of the Four Rivers. It is decorated with sculptures of four river gods that represent four of the world's major rivers – the Nile, the Danube, the Ganges, and the Río de la Plata. I'm off for a quick splash!

The river god of the Ganges River is holding an oar to represent that it is an easy river to sail down.

Trevi Fountain

According to legend, if you toss a coin into the Trevi Fountain, you'll return to Rome someday.

That must be why my grandma included a coin in her travel journal. She knew one trip to Rome wouldn't be enough for me! Let's take a closer look at this beautiful and massive fountain. It was built in the 1700's in the Baroque style. This style of architecture is dramatic and large, with lots of details and movement. It's hard to believe that the statues in the middle are made of stone ... they are so realistic! The figure in the center is Oceanus – an ancient Roman god who was connected to a mystical river that encircled the world.

This strange animal is a mythical creature that is half horse, half fish. It's being guided by a triton – a Greek sea god.

The water in the Trevi Fountain comes from a Roman aqueduct (an artificial channel that carries water) called the Aqua Virgo. In Roman times, there were many aqueducts that transported drinking water from the surrounding mountains to the city. The Aqua Virgo is the only one that remains today. It also supplies water to other fountains around the city.

The coins thrown into the Trevi Fountain are collected daily and donated to charity.

Spanish Steps

Wow! That's a lot of steps! 135 to be precise.

The Spanish Steps connect the Piazza de Spagna square at the bottom with the Trinità dei Monti church at the top. Confusingly, the steps don't have anything to do with Spain at all! A French diplomat actually paid for the construction of the steps in the 1720's. However, at that time, the Spanish embassy was located in the Piazza de Spagna at the base of the steps and over time, the steps became known as the Spanish Steps.

The steps are a very popular tourist attraction and are often crowded with people. Take your time and wander slowly to the top. If you need a break, there are three terraces where you can stop and look out over your progress so far. However, you aren't allowed to sit on the steps, so don't get too comfortable! Instead, head down into the Piazza de Spagna for a drink or a gelato. There is even a traditional English tearoom in the square, where you can sip tea and nibble on cakes and pastries.

Villa Borghese

Wow! What a massive park! These gardens used to belong to a huge mansion called the Villa Borghese.

They were bought by the Italian government at the beginning of the 1900's and opened as a public park. Locals love to come here to stroll around, ride bikes, or even rent boats and row across the lake! Its hills, meadows, and woods seem like natural countryside.

But there's much more to this park than just walking and exploring. Do you remember the Villa Borghese mansion I mentioned earlier? Well, that building is home to a massive art gallery. It's my next stop after these gardens!

There are also several other villas, a replica of Shakespeare's Globe Theatre from the 1500's, and a water clock. If I have time, I want to visit the Bioparco. This is a zoo with a focus on conservation. They have around 1,200 animals from more than 150 different species, including Asian elephants, wolves, and green anacondas! No puffins though ...

Borghese Gallery

That's right! You can't come to the Villa Borghese gardens and not visit the villa itself. Inside the villa is a huge art museum called the Borghese Gallery.

The villa was built at the beginning of the 1600's under the instruction of Scipione Borghese, a member of the noble Borghese family. Scipione's uncle was the pope at that time. This made the Borghese family even more powerful and wealthy. Scipione was very interested in the arts. He collected ancient and famous artwork, and paid artists to create new paintings and sculptures for his collection. Villa Borghese was built to store and display Scipione's huge art collection.

You can still see a lot of Scipione's art collection in the Borghese Gallery today. There are rooms filled with ancient Roman sculptures and mosaics, as well as many paintings and sculptures by famous artists. Even the walls and ceilings of the rooms are painted with beautiful designs! Which exhibits would you like to visit first?

These painted wall and ceiling murals are known as frescoes. The artist painted straight on to the plaster covering the wall.
Even the outside of the Villa Borghese is decorated with sculptures and designs!
Where's that beautiful music coming from?

Parco della Musica

The Parco della Musica isn't in my grandma's journal, as it only opened in 2002.

I'm going to add my own journal entry about it so that future generations will know to visit this incredible music venue when they visit Rome. You can tell that Parco della Musica was built recently, as it looks very modern. It was designed by Italian architect Renzo Piano. I've seen other buildings by Renzo Piano on my travels, such as the Shard in London, United Kingdom, and the Centre Pompidou in Paris, France.

The three pods each hold a large concert hall. There's also an outdoor performance space with room for over 3,000 people in the audience. It reminds me a bit of a Roman amphitheater, like the Colosseum! This isn't the only connection between the past and the present here at the Parco della Musica. During its construction, builders discovered the remains of a Roman farmhouse. Renzo Piano and his team changed their plans for the Parco della Musica to include the Roman ruins.

The Roman ruins on the site of Parco della Musica have been excavated and left uncovered, so you can learn about history and listen to a concert in one trip!

You can listen to many types of music at the Parco della Musica, including music by Italian composers, jazz, and modern music.

Castel Sant'Angelo

The Castel Sant'Angelo has been many things over the years – a resting place for Roman emperors, a fortress, a barracks where soldiers live, and finally, a museum!

It was built in the A.D. 130's as a mausoleum (building where dead people are buried) for the Roman emperor Hadrian and his family. Later, the remains of other Roman emperors were also placed here. At this point, it was just a tall, round tower.

There are lots of angel statues around the Castel Sant'Angelo because it is named after an important Christian angel.

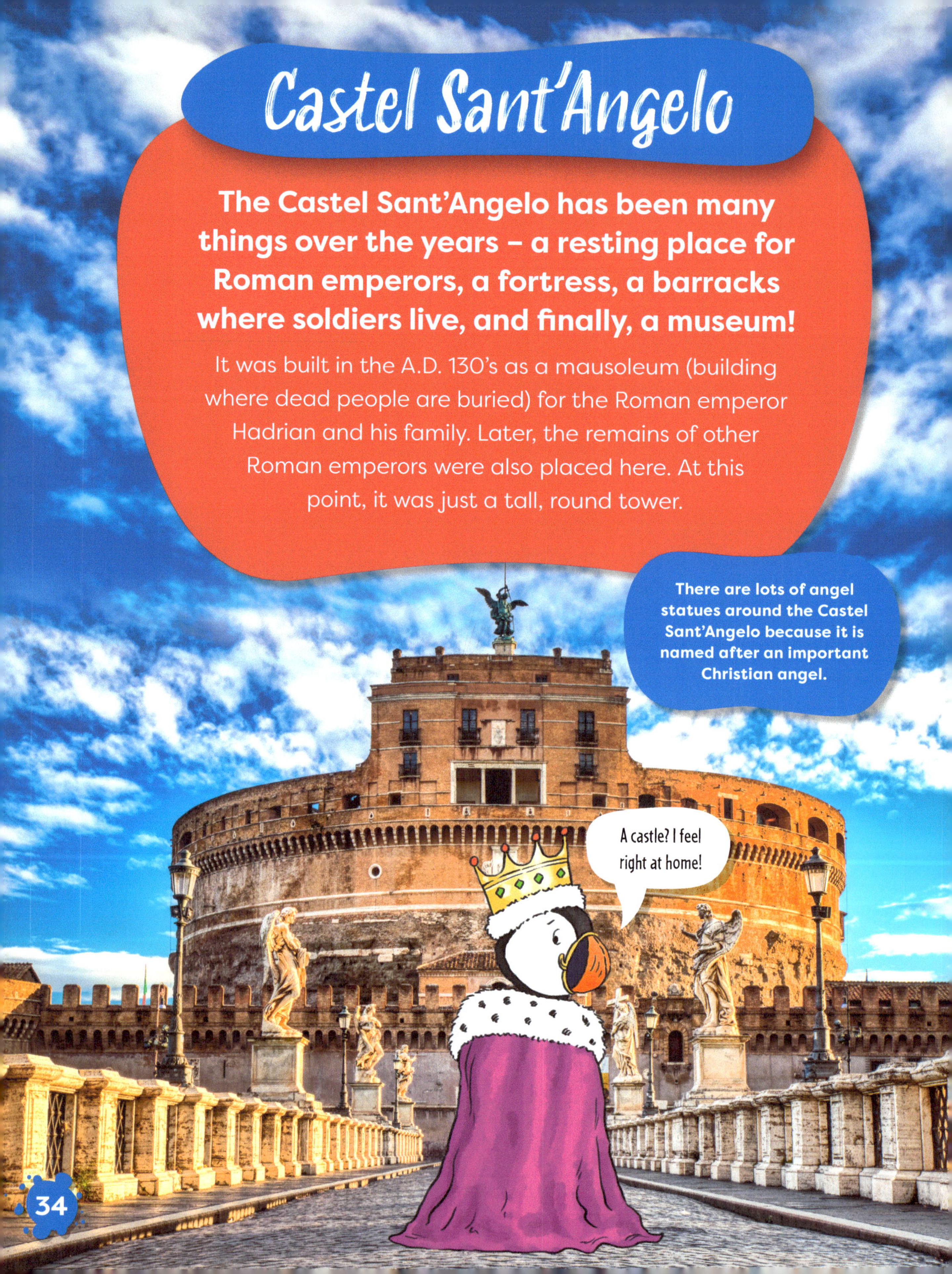

The Castel Sant'Angelo lies on the banks of the Tiber River, next to an ancient Roman bridge. Emperor Hadrian had the bridge built to connect his mausoleum to the city center. The bridge was later named the Ponte Sant'Angelo after the castle.

In the 400's, the building was turned into a fortress. They built square walls around the central tower. In the Middle Ages, more protection was added to the building, making it a castle. It became a safe place for important people, such as the pope, to shelter during attacks on the city. The pope escaped into the castle through a protected corridor that was connected to Vatican City. The castle was also used as a prison, and later a barracks. In 1901, the barracks closed and the castle building was restored. Today, it's a museum where you can explore the building for yourself and learn more about its dramatic history!

Vatican City

Did you know that there's an entire country inside the city of Rome?

Within the city of Rome is Vatican City – the smallest independent country in the world and the home of the Roman Catholic Church. The entire country covers just 0.17 square miles (0.44 square kilometers) – about the size of an average city park.

Despite its small size, the country is packed full of incredible buildings and is home to one of the world's largest churches, a huge palace, many priceless artworks, and much, much more!

My trip within a trip begins in St. Peter's Square, outside St. Peter's Basilica. At the moment I'm still in Italy, but as soon as I enter the square, I'll be in another country! St. Peter's Basilica is built on top of the tomb believed to hold the body of Saint Peter, the first pope. The church is built in the shape of a cross. Its striking dome was designed by the great artist and architect Michelangelo (more on him in a minute!). It rises 400 feet (121 meters) above the floor of the church.

The interior of St. Peter's Basilica is decorated with sculptures, mosaics, and paintings, with touches of gold.

The Sistine Chapel is part of the palace in the Vatican. It looks simple on the outside, but inside, it's like stepping into a giant work of art. Its walls and ceiling are decorated with incredible paintings by some of the greatest artists of the late 1400's and early 1500's. The paintings show the history of the world according to the Bible. Do you remember Michelangelo, who designed the dome of St. Peter's Basilica? He painted many parts of the Sistine Chapel, including its massive ceiling.

The Sistine Chapel is an important place for the Roman Catholic Church. Cardinals (high-ranking members of the church who advise the pope) meet here to vote for a new pope if a pope dies or resigns. Other important ceremonies are also held here.

Michelangelo used scaffolding to reach the ceiling of the Sistine Chapel. It took him four years to paint the ceiling alone!

There are around 20,000 different works of art on display across the Vatican Museums, including ancient Greek and Roman sculptures, items from ancient Egypt, and religious paintings.
This room contains so many statues of animals, it's known as the "stone zoo"! I wonder if there's a statue of a puffin here!
I guess I'm headed across the river next!
Across the Tiber
Vatican City doesn't have an army or a navy. However, the Swiss Guard (a group of Swiss soldiers) protects the pope and the Vatican Palace.
The Swiss Guard's uniforms haven't changed much since they started protecting the pope in the late 1400's!

Trastevere

Welcome to Trastevere! The name of this Roman neighborhood comes from the Latin for "across the Tiber," so I know I'm in the right place.

In Roman times, few buildings were located on this side of the Tiber River. During the Roman Republic, this was a multicultural area, home to sailors and immigrants from other countries. Later, in the Middle Ages, rich and powerful people lived here in palaces. Now, it's a popular place to eat and drink.

There is still lots of character from the past in Trastevere. I'm having a great time walking around the cobbled streets, exploring the narrow alleyways, and spotting old buildings. You never know what you might find around the next corner! So far, I've found fountains, villas, and some of the oldest churches in Rome! The site of the Basilica di Santa Maria in Trastevere has been used as a Christian place of worship since A.D. 434.

The inside of the Basilica di Santa Maria in Trastevere is decorated with intricate mosaics and striking gold details.

My stomach is starting to rumble, so it's time to find some food.

Many people have tried Italian food before, but you may not have had the chance to try traditional Roman food. I can't wait to try it for myself!

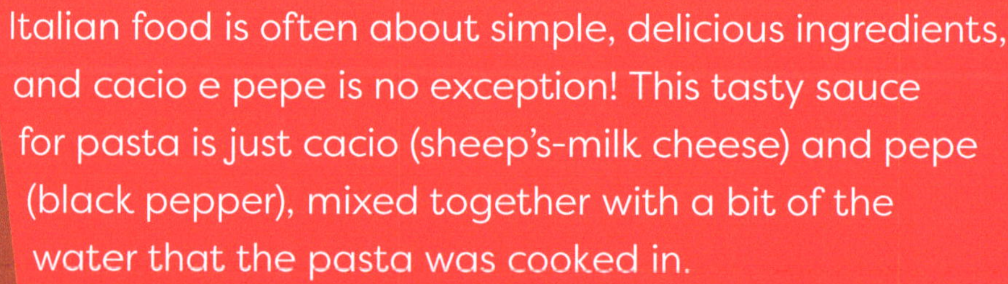

Italian food is often about simple, delicious ingredients, and cacio e pepe is no exception! This tasty sauce for pasta is just cacio (sheep's-milk cheese) and pepe (black pepper), mixed together with a bit of the water that the pasta was cooked in.

Deep-fried artichokes started out in Rome's Jewish community, but today they are a popular springtime dish for all Romans! The outer leaves are crunchy, like chips, and the inside is buttery and rich.

Can't decide which type of pizza you want? Grab some pizza al taglio! This pizza is sold by the slice, so you can try as many different flavors as you like! The slices are rectangular, rather than the wedge shape you might be used to.

Chocolate? Vanilla? Or maybe something more unusual like avocado, celery, or even gorgonzola cheese! Whether you like the more traditional flavors or something more modern, there's gelato for everyone in Rome. But be warned if you ask for a cone – some stores will only serve their gelato in a cup because they think the flavor of the cone distracts from the flavor of their gelato!

Yum! This pizza is amazing! I've had a terrific time exploring Rome, thanks to my grandma's helpful suggestions and notes. I've added some more places to her journal so the next generation of traveling puffins will know all the best spots to visit on their trip to Rome. Ciao for now!

ROME
- MAP -
Parco della
Musica
Tiber River
Castel Sant'Angelo
Vatican City
Piazza
Navona
Trastevere

Villa Borghese

Spanish Steps

Trevi Fountain

Pantheon

Roman Forum

Colosseum

Vittoriano

Circus Maximus

Palatine Hill

A Day in Rome

What a beautiful morning in Rome! Make sure you wear good walking shoes for your travels around this historic city.

First stop: the Roman Colosseum! Climb the tiers and imagine what it would have been like to be a gladiator in this massive amphitheater.

Take a stroll over to Trevi Fountain and admire the Baroque architecture from the 1700's. The stone carvings are so detailed!

Make sure to toss a coin in the fountain in hopes of returning to Rome someday!

Next up are the Spanish Steps. It's a bit of a hike to the top, so feel free to rest a bit at Piazza de Spagna before you begin your trek.

Cold and creamy gelato sounds like the perfect treat!

The architecture in Rome is quite impressive, but you must check out some artwork, too! Make your way to the Borghese Gallery, where you'll see ancient Roman sculptures and mosaics as well as famous paintings from Rome's more recent history.

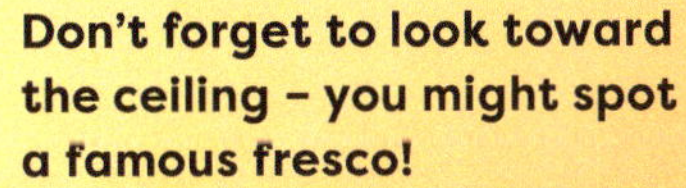

Don't forget to look toward the ceiling – you might spot a famous fresco!

End your busy day in Rome by crossing the Tiber River. Enjoy a walk through the picturesque Trastevere neighborhood before finding a restaurant for a traditional Roman dinner. Mangia!

Where Am I?

Destination 1

This destination sits on top of an ancient circus where today's visitors can tour the underground ruins.

In the past, this square was flooded as part of a celebration to honor the Pamphili family.

Today, this square has three fountains, including the famous Fountain of the Four Rivers.

Destination 2

This destination was home to the most important public spaces during both the Roman Republic and Roman Empire.

Ancient Romans drained a massive swamp in order to build on this land.

Today, visitors can admire the beauty and strength of Roman architecture by exploring the ruins.

Destination 3

Visitors can see more than 20,000 works of art across this destination's many museums.

The great artist and architect Michelangelo designed parts of St. Peter's Basilica and the Sistine Chapel, both important buildings located here.

This destination is home to the Roman Catholic Church and is the world's smallest independent country.

Destination 4

In the past, people built villas, palaces, and temples here. Today, visitors can see their ruins.

This destination is located in the center of Rome's seven hills and is one of the oldest parts of the city.

According to ancient legend, this location housed Romulus and Remus, the founders of Rome who were looked after by a female wolf.

Destination 5

Visitors can listen to music in one of the three concert halls or in an outdoor amphitheater.

This modern music venue opened in 2002.

During construction, builders discovered ruins from an ancient Roman farmhouse, which are now on display.

Destination 6

Many people refer to this destination as the "wedding cake" because of its levels.

Visitors can view the Tomb of the Unknown Soldier and pay tribute to those who were killed or went missing during wars.

This monument was built to honor King Victor Emmanuel II, the first king of a united Italy.

Answers on page 55

Photos from Rome

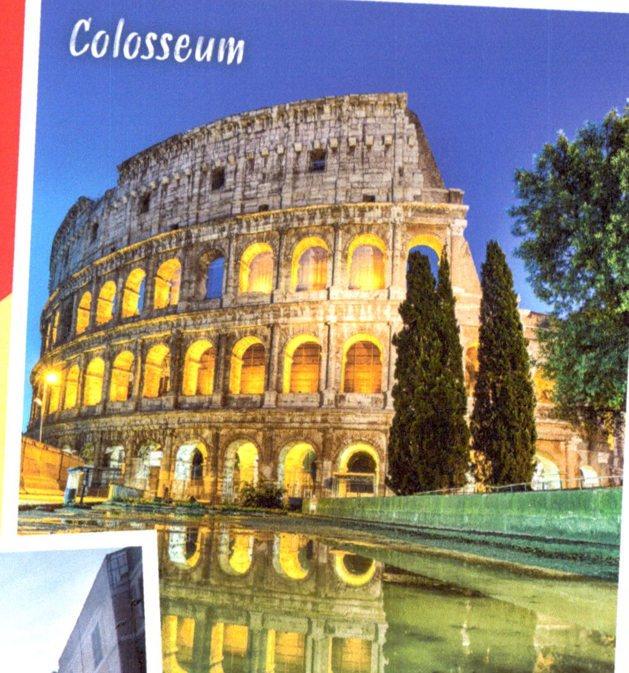
Colosseum

Piazza de Spagna

Fountain of the Four Rivers

Pantheon

Trevi Fountain

Basilica di Santa Maria

Castel Sant'Angelo

Engage Your Reader

Activate background knowledge, set the purpose for reading, and monitor comprehension with this tried-and-true reading strategy!

Work with your reader(s) to create a KWL chart. Take some time to discuss what students already KNOW about Rome as well as what they WONDER about the city. You will revisit what they LEARNED after reading the book.

KNOW	WONDER	LEARNED

1. Have readers preview the structure of this text by flipping through the pages. Page 5 describes how clues are included for Norrie's next destinations.
2. Set the tone for reading: *As you read, think about all the different places in Rome and how history, culture, and people have shaped them into what they are today.*
3. After reading each section, revisit the KWL chart. Brainstorm what readers LEARNED from this section and add it to the chart. Your reader can add other wonderings they may have had, too!

Consider these questions to guide the brainstorming process:

- Why is location important to places, history, and culture?
- What patterns do you notice in the placement of things around the city of Rome?
- What makes Rome unique?

Use these comprehension questions to help your reader(s) check their understanding as they navigate the text.

p. 6-7 What did Palatine Hill look like during the Roman Empire? What does it look like today?

p. 8-9 In what ways were the buildings of the Roman Forum used between 590 B.C. and A.D. 476?

p. 10-11 When and why was the arch shown on page 11 first constructed?

p. 12-13 What was the Temple of Vesta?

Why was it considered a great honor to be chosen as a Vestal Virgin?

p. 14-15 How has the world-famous Roman Colosseum been used over time?

p. 16-17 What types of events took place at Circus Maximus during ancient times?

p. 18-19 Who was King Victor Emmanuel II?

p. 20-21 Why is the Pantheon so well preserved in comparison to other ancient Roman buildings?

Why did Roman architects begin building domes?

p. 22-23 Why was Piazza Navona flooded on Saturdays and Sundays in August between 1652 and 1866?

p. 24-25 According to legend, what is said to happen to those who toss coins into the Trevi Fountain?

Where are those coins taken at the end of each day?

p. 26-27 How did the Spanish Steps get their name?

p. 28-29 What would you enjoy most about a visit to Villa Borghese?

p. 30-31 Why was the Borghese Gallery first built?

What art can visitors see today?

p. 32-33 How does the modern Parco della Musica, built in 2002, relate to Rome's history?

p. 34-35 How has Castel Sant'Angelo been used over time?

p. 36-37 Vatican City is the smallest independent country in the world! For what else is this 0.17 square miles of land known?

p. 38-39 What does the Sistine Chapel look like? Why is it an important building?

p. 40-41 How has the Trastevere neighborhood changed over time?

p. 42-43 Of all the food described here, what would you most like to try? Why?

Extend Through Writing

Norrie the puffin just took you on a tour of Rome, Italy! Based on the places highlighted in this book, where would you like to visit in Rome?

Your written response should include:

- An introduction, including a general statement about Rome
- At least three places you would like to visit and at least three reasons why these places interest you
- A conclusion in which you briefly restate your interest in these three famous Rome destinations

Copy this graphic organizer onto another sheet of paper or visit **www.worldbook.com/resources** to download and print a copy. Use it to help you plan your writing.

<table>
<tr><td colspan="3">Introduction:</td></tr>
<tr><td>Destination 1</td><td>Destination 2</td><td>Destination 3</td></tr>
<tr><td>Reason 1</td><td>Reason 1</td><td>Reason 1</td></tr>
<tr><td>Reason 2</td><td>Reason 2</td><td>Reason 2</td></tr>
<tr><td>Reason 3</td><td>Reason 3</td><td>Reason 3</td></tr>
<tr><td colspan="3">Conclusion:</td></tr>
</table>

Answers

Where Am I? answers, p. 48-49:

1. Piazza Navona, 2. Roman Forum, 3. Vatican City, 4. Palatine Hill, 5. Parco della Musica, 6. Vittoriano

Comprehension question answers, p. 53:

p. 6-7

During the Roman Empire, Palatine Hill was home to huge villas, palaces, and temples. Today, visitors can see the ruins of these ancient buildings.

p. 8-9

Roman Forum buildings were used as government houses as well as for processions and religious ceremonies.

p. 10-11

The massive arch highlighted on page 11 was constructed in A.D. 203, over 2,000 years ago! It celebrated the Roman victory of Emperor Septimius Severus over the Parthian Empire.

p. 12-13

The Temple of Vesta was dedicated to the Roman goddess of the home and hearth. It was a great honor to be chosen as a Vestal Virgin because these six priestesses were in charge of ensuring the temple's flame never went out in hopes of protecting Rome.

p. 14-15

When the Roman Colosseum was first built, it was a massive amphitheater where people gathered to watch gladiator fights and wild animal hunts. It has also been used as a burial ground, fortress, housing, and a holy place. Today, it is a major tourist attraction.

p. 16-17

Circus Maximus could hold up to 250,000 spectators. In the past, it hosted chariot and horse races. Today, it is a concert venue.

p. 18-19

King Victor Emmanuel II was the first king of a united Italy. His statue is located at the famous Vittoriano on Capitoline Hill.

p. 20-21

The Pantheon is considered better preserved than many other ancient Roman buildings because it has always been in use.

Roman architects began constructing domed roofs because they wanted buildings that were open on the inside without being cluttered by columns.

p. 22-23

Piazza Navona was flooded on weekends in August between 1652 and 1866 as part of a festival to celebrate the rich and powerful Pamphili family.

p. 24-25

According to legend, tossing a coin into the Trevi Fountain will ensure you return to the city of Rome.

At the end of each day, the coins are collected and donated to charity.

p. 26-27

Despite these famous steps being paid for by a French diplomat, they gained their name because the Spanish embassy to Italy was located at their base when they were first constructed.

p. 28-29

Answers may vary.

p. 30-31

The Borghese Gallery was first built to house Scipione Borghese's collection of artwork. Today, visitors can see pieces from his collection, as well as other famous paintings, sculptures, and mosaics. Visitors can also see frescoes, murals painted directly on the walls and ceilings!

p. 32-33

The modern Parco della Musica connects to Rome's history because builders discovered the remains of a Roman farmhouse during construction. In addition, it contains an amphitheater as a nod to the Colosseum.

p. 34-35

Castel Sant'Angelo was originally constructed as a mausoleum, but it has also been used as a fortress, barracks for soldiers, and a shelter for such important figures as the pope. Today, it is a popular museum.

p. 36-37

Vatican City is home to the Roman Catholic Church. It is known for its architecture, huge palace, and famous artwork, among other things.

p. 38-39

The Sistine Chapel is a simple building from the outside, but its walls and ceilings are decorated with some of the world's most famous paintings. Michelangelo designed and painted the fresco on the chapel's massive ceiling.

p. 40-41

During the Roman Republic, the Trastevere neighborhood was home to many sailors and immigrants. Powerful people moved into the neighborhood's palaces during the Middle Ages. Today, people visit this area for delicious food and drinks.

p. 42-43

Answers may vary.

Glossary

amphitheater *(AM fuh THEE uh tuhr)* A circular or oval building with rows of seats around a central open space

aqueduct *(AK wuh duhkt)* An artificial channel that carries water

basilica *(buh SIHL uh kuh)* An oblong hall with a row of columns at each side (separating the high main portion from the side aisles) and a structure in the shape of a half circle at one end, or sometimes at both ends

circus *(SUR kuhs)* A round, oval, or oblong space with seats around it in rows, each row higher than the one in front of it

emperor *(EHM per ohr)* The ruler of a large area, sometimes a group of nations or states

excavation *(EHKS kuh VAY shuhn)* The act or process of digging out or up

fresco *(FREHS koh)* A painting on damp plaster

mausoleum *(MAW suh LEE uhm)* A large, magnificent tomb, especially one above ground

mosaic *(moh ZAY ihk)* Pictures or decorations made with small pieces of colored glass or stone

Vatican *(VAT ih kuhn)* A short name for Vatican City; the pope and the government of Vatican City

Index

www.ingramcontent.com/pod-product-compliance
Ingram Content Group UK Ltd.
Pitfield, Milton Keynes, MK11 3LW, UK
UKHW060105300726
14090UKWH00003B/379

* 9 7 8 0 7 1 6 6 5 3 3 0 1 *